Do You Know Your Wife?

A Quiz about the Woman in Your Life

DAN CARLINSKY

 sourcebooks

 $\mathcal{T}$ hink you know all about the woman on the other side of the dinner table? Well, maybe. Let this little book be the judge.

If the two of you are like most couples, you probably talk more about the neighbors and the news than about yourselves. The result: an information gap.

Counselors say that knowing about your partner's past and preferences can be important—even things like "Who was her best friend in grade school?" and "Does she hate squash?" Knowing, they say—even knowing such bits of trivia—is a sign of caring.

So grab a pencil and show what you know. The answers, of course, are not in the book; only she can say. So after you've completed the test, ask her to check your answers and figure your score.

The test has 100 questions. Count ten points for each correct answer. Where you miss some of a multipart question, divide and take partial credit; you'll need all the help you can get. Here's how to rate yourself:

> **Above 900:** Very impressive. In fact, downright amazing.
>
> **700–900:** Pretty good, but there's still room for improvement.
>
> **Below 700:** Weak. Ask him to give you a remedial course.

You may find you have something to brag about, or you may be humbled. Either way, just by going over your answers together, you'll learn a little and have some fun as well. Good luck.

—D.C.

1. **For starters, will she take this test:**

   ____ Eagerly?

   ____ Indifferently?

   ____ Kicking and screaming?

2. **Does she usually carry enough cash to:**

   ____ Buy a cup of coffee?

   ____ Cover lunch for herself?

   ____ Treat a crowd to dinner and then some?

3. **When she has a headache, does she usually take:**

   ____ An aspirin?   ____ Another pain medication?

   ____ Two aspirin?   ____ Nothing?

4. **Did she ever win a contest of any sort? If so, what was her prize?**

   ____ Yes, she won: _____.

   ____ No

5. **What's her favorite color?**

6. **When dressing for an evening out, does she put on makeup:**

   ____ Early in the process?

   ____ Last thing?

   ____ Not at all?

7. **Within two, how many keys does she carry?**

8. **Which item of clothing of yours does she really like?**

9. **If you want to make her unhappy, serve her:**

   _____ for dinner.

10. **Who's her favorite singer?**

11. How often does she generally shop for groceries?

_____ Once a week or less

_____ Twice a week

_____ Three times a week or more

12. If her best friend passed along a juicy piece of gossip and warned her not to tell a soul, would she tell you?

_____ Absolutely not

_____ She might

_____ She probably would

_____ Of course

13. What was her telephone number when you first met?

14. When she was a little girl, what was her answer when people asked, "What do you want to be when you grow up?"

15. If she had a chance to have her fortune told for free, would she:

_____ Accept and heed the fortune-teller's words?

_____ Accept but treat the whole thing as a joke?

_____ Decline because she thinks such stuff is nonsense?

16. Has she kept any object—a book, a toy, a doll—since childhood?

_____ Yes, _____.

_____ No

17. It's late at night. The phone rings. She answers and hears heavy breathing, then a string of obscenities. What does she do?

_____ Panic

_____ Hang up and go back to sleep

_____ Keep listening

_____ Yell at the caller

_____ Laugh

_____ Hand the receiver to you

18. How old was she on her first date?

19. **When she comes home to an empty house, does she immediately turn on a radio or television?**

____ Yes   ____ No

20. Do you know her feet? Check the appropriate line.

____ Her left foot is slightly larger than her right.

____ Her right foot is slightly larger than her left.

____ As far as she can tell, they're the same size.

21. If the washing machine broke down, what would she do?

____ Fix it   ____ Call you

____ Call a repairman   ____ Wait until you got home

22. At a picnic, would she rather drink:

____ Beer?   ____ Water?

____ Cocktail?   ____ Iced tea?

____ Wine?   ____ Soft drink?

23. Has she ever bought a lottery ticket?

____ Yes   ____ No

24. What's her favorite place to buy clothes?

25. Does she send a photo to a friend (or you) at least once a week?

_____ Yes   _____ No

26. If you wanted to surprise her by making reservations at her favorite restaurant, which place should you call?

27. Approximately how many books has she read in the past year?

_____ None   _____ Two to five

_____ One   _____ More than five

28. Does she ever read cookbooks just for fun?

_____ Yes   _____ No

29. Does she ever invent her own recipes?

_____ Often   _____ Never

_____ Sometimes

30. What's her mother's maiden name?

31. What's her parents' street address?

32. If she's served chicken, she'll reach first for:

_____ White meat

_____ Dark meat

_____ Either

_____ Something other than chicken

33. What piece of furniture—in any room—would she most like to replace?

34. Does she keep a photo of you:

_____ In her wallet?   _____ At work?

35. Who was her favorite Beatle?

_____ John   _____ Ringo

_____ Paul   _____ George

_____ Favorite what?

36. Has she ever used a power saw?

_____ Yes   _____ No

37. If you two had to move out of the country, where would she choose to go?

38. What's the one television program she can't do without?

39. If a volunteer from a charity knocked on the door and asked for a contribution, what would she do?

_____ Make a token gift

_____ Give more

_____ Politely decline

_____ Say no and shut the door

40. What color is her everyday handbag or backpack?

41. Did she have a TV in her bedroom when she was a kid?

_____ Yes   _____ No

42. Would she donate a kidney to:

_____ A close relative?

_____ A close friend?

_____ You?

43. Does she know who Pythagoras was?

_____ Yes   _____ No

44. Given a well-stocked fruit bowl, which would she most likely choose first?

_____ Apple

_____ Banana

_____ Orange

_____ Grapes

_____ Pear

_____ None—she'd look for a doughnut

45. How often does she wash her hair?

_____ Daily   _____ Twice a week

_____ Every other day   _____ No more than weekly

46. What would she say about the idea of a strip club a mile from your home?

____ "Where do I sign to protest?"

____ "Makes no difference to me."

____ "Great!"

____ "Hmm. I wonder if they're hiring."

47. When she passes a mirror when out and about, what does she usually do?

____ Glance at her reflection and keep walking

____ Stop and inspect herself very carefully

____ Ignore the glass and go on her way

48. Which would she rather do?

____ Wash dishes   ____ Dry dishes

49. Which would she prefer?

____ A full-time maid   ____ Neither (honestly)

____ A full-time cook

50. What's her favorite flower? (Five bonus points if you know the color too.)

51. Does she think most stand-up comics are funny?

____ Yes   ____ Sort of

____ No

52. Where would she rather vacation?

____ In a private mountain cabin

____ At a beach resort

____ Any place with good shopping

____ A place with great shows

____ A foreign country with history

____ At home in peace and quiet

53. What jewelry does she wear just hanging out at home?

____ Engagement ring   ____ Bracelet(s)

____ Wedding band   ____ Earrings

____ Other ring(s)   ____ Anything else

54. How does she like most meat?

____ Rare   ____ Medium well

____ Medium rare   ____ Well-done

____ Medium   ____ She doesn't

55. Name at least two of her old teachers. (Any grade will do.)

56. Will she say she gets her news mostly from newspapers, TV, internet news sites, or social media?

57. How many credit cards does she have?

_____ None

_____ One to three

_____ Four to six

_____ More

58. Does she close the bathroom door when no one else is home?

_____ Yes

No

59. Does she know the first names of at least two of her great-grandparents?

_____ Yes

_____ No

60. When shopping for clothes, does she prefer:

_____ To browse and ask questions only when necessary?

_____ To be helped by a salesperson from the start?

61. Can she name a currently active professional:

_____ Golfer?

_____ Tennis player?

_____ Jockey?

62. Does she know the capital of Argentina?

_____ Yes   _____ No

63. Can she touch her elbows together behind her back?

_____ Yes   _____ No

64. Has she ever shot with a bow and arrow?

_____ Yes   _____ No

65. When was she at her lifetime high weight? (Or is she at her heaviest right now?)

66. In which financial category would she place her family when she was growing up?

_____ Rich   _____ Just managing

_____ Comfortable   _____ Really struggling

67. If offered some chocolate-covered termites as a "delicacy," she would:

_____ Try some out of genuine interest

_____ Try some to be polite

_____ Gently decline, explaining that the thought doesn't appeal to her

_____ Make up an excuse like "Sorry, I'm dieting"

68. If she saw one of her favorite movie actors on the street, would she:

_____ Pretend she didn't notice?

_____ Nod or say hello and keep walking?

_____ Politely ask for an autograph?

_____ Try to start a conversation?

69. If she developed a terminal illness, would she:

_____ Want to know about it in detail?

_____ Want to know just the basics?

_____ Prefer not to be told?

70. Did she have a childhood nickname?

_____ Yes, the kids called her _____.

_____ No

71. If she could name her job, what would she want to do?

72. How does she use salt at the table?

_____ Adds it to some foods before tasting

_____ Adds it only after tasting

_____ Rarely or never uses it

73. Which of these can't she do?

_____ Touch her toes   _____ Jump-start a car

_____ Stand on her head   _____ Rewire a lamp

74. Which statement best expresses her thinking?

_____ "Most women are better off married."

_____ "Most women are better off single."

_____ She wouldn't make either blanket statement.

75. What's her favorite holiday?

76. She always carries:

_____ Her phone

_____ Her keys

_____ Tissues

_____ A snack

_____ Water

77. Does she have any major regrets in her life that are frequently on her mind?

_____ Yes: _____

_____

_____ No

78. She usually falls asleep:

_____ As soon as her head hits the pillow

_____ Within a few minutes

_____ With great difficulty

79. If she went away for several days and returned to find that you had made a dramatic change in your appearance (grew a beard, dyed your hair), what would she most likely do?

_____ Be annoyed that you didn't ask for her opinion first

_____ Compliment you

_____ Laugh

80. "There's nothing wrong with separate vacations. In fact, it's not a bad idea at all." Will she:

____ Agree?

____ Disagree?

81. If she came into a lot of money, in what order would she rank these possible uses for the cash?

____ Debts

____ Dream purchases

____ Family

____ Friends

____ Charities

82. Without looking, tell how she parts her hair.

____ On the left   ____ In the center

____ On the right   ____ Not at all

83. Would she rather be buried or cremated?

____ Buried   ____ No opinion

____ Cremated

84. Does she own a blue coat?

____ Yes   ____ No

85. When did she most recently chew bubble gum?

_____ Very recently

_____ Within the past year or so

_____ A few years back

_____ Many years ago, if ever

86. Does she doodle while talking on the phone?

_____ Often

_____ Sometimes

_____ Never

87. How many cups of coffee or tea does she drink in a typical day?

_____ None

_____ One to three

_____ Four to six

_____ Seven or more

88. If, for some reason, you two had to attend an hour-long musical skit performed by a group of children, not one of them related to you, would she:

_____ Enjoy herself?

_____ Tolerate the show?

_____ Claw at the seat until the thing was over?

89. Is there any skill you have that she'd like you to teach her?

_____ Yes: _____.

_____ No

90. Of her married friends, who does she think picked the best partner?

91. When she gets something new, does she generally:

_____ Use it right away?

_____ Save it for later?

92. "A person with good vision who wears dark glasses indoors is either pretentious or a little crazy." Would she:

_____ Agree?

_____ Disagree?

_____ Decline to give a simple yes or no?

_____ Have no opinion?

93. Has she bought anything online or from a TV shopping show within the past year?

_____ Yes   _____ No

94. Does she believe in a personal god who intervenes in human affairs?

____ Yes ____ She can't say

____ No

95. Does she have a favorite scent?

____ Yes: _____

____ No

96. Which color or colors does she think you look best in?

97. Can she sing any school song from her alma mater?

____ Yes

____ No, but she can hum the tune

____ She can't remember it at all

98. If she were going to get a new pet tomorrow, what kind of animal would she want? And what breed?

99. What's her favorite movie of the past five years?

100. Can she name the current secretary general of the United Nations?

_____ Yes, easily

_____ Yes, after some thought

_____ She'll come close

_____ No way

Published by Sourcebooks
P.O. Box 4410, Naperville, Illinois 60567-4410
(630) 961-3900
sourcebooks.com

Library of Congress Cataloging-in-Publication data is on file with the publisher

Printed and bound in the United States of America.

DR 10 9 8 7 6 5 4 3 2 1